BOLD KIDS

MW01252373

Indonesia

A VARIETY OF FACTS
CHILDREN'S PEOPLE AND PLACES BOOK

If you're wondering what Indonesia has to offer, you may want to learn a few facts about the country. The country of 17508 islands is a republic, has a large young population, and is home to a large number of active volcanoes.

You might even be surprised to learn that Indonesia has one of the highest literacy rates in the world.

INDONESIA IS A COUNTRY OF 17000+ ISLANDS

Indonesia is an archipelagic country of 17000 islands, the largest in the world. Of these islands, about 6,200 are inhabited.

Its strategic position on the sea-lanes of Southeast Asia have facilitated inter-island and international trade, which has fundamentally shaped its history. It is also home to a diverse population of ethnic and cultural groups from diverse migrations.

Indonesia's largest islands are the Java Archipelago, Sumatra, and Kalimantan. It is also home to more than 7,000 smaller islands, including Papua, New Guinea, and Timor-Leste.

Most of these islands are covered in dense rain forests and some of them have active volcanoes.

IT IS A REPUBLIC

Indonesia is a nation in Southeast Asia. It was colonized by the Dutch in the early 17th century and was occupied by the Japanese during the second world war.

The Japanese occupied Indonesia and a small group of Indonesians, led by Sukarno, declared independence unilaterally on August 17, 1945.

Sukarno became the first president of Indonesia and Muhammad Hatta became vice president. After the war, the Dutch attempted to retake the island but were beaten back.

The Dutch finally acknowledged Indonesia's independence in 1949.

The government of Indonesia is based on a 1945 constitution that provides limited separation of executive, legislative, and judicial powers. However, the country has undergone significant restructuring since the resignation of former President Soeharto and the emergence of the new government of President Habibie.

Habibie's government passed legislation to reform the country's political system. Though these legislative reforms did not alter the Indonesian constitution, they created a new electoral system and political parties.

IT HAS A LARGE NUMBER OF ACTIVE VOLCANOES

The country of Indonesia has an abundance of active volcanoes, with 197 million people living within 100 kilometres of one.

It is located within the Pacific Ring of Fire, which spans 40,000 km or 25,000 miles from South America through the North Pacific, to Japan and New Zealand. More than half of the volcanoes in this region are active. This makes Indonesia one of the most active areas in the world.

One of the most active volcanoes in Indonesia is the Sinabung volcano, which woke up in 2010 after a 400-year sleep.

Since then, it has erupted continuously, producing ash plumes up to 11 kilometers into the atmosphere and ash and pyroclastic deposits up to a kilometer high. This active volcano has caused significant damage and has killed at least 25 people.

IT HAS SOME OF THE BEST FOOD IN THE WORLD

The cuisine of Indonesia is known for its rice, which is cooked with a variety of ingredients. Popular dishes include Nasi Goreng, which is eaten for breakfast. It is often served with a sunny side egg, prawn crackers, and cucumber pickles.

Another famous Indonesian dish is Pepes, which is made by steaming meat inside banana leaves. Indonesian cuisine is based on plant-based ingredients, with many local vegetables. The country has ample agricultural lands, and its traditional plant-based dishes make the most of these crops.

CPSIA information can be obtained
at www.ICGtesting.com
Printed in the USA
LVHW072332250123
737950LV00022B/1553